SPOOKY RIDDLES

Marc Brown

BEGINNER BOOKS
A Division of Random House, Inc.

Library of Congress Cataloging in Publication Data: Brown, Marc Tolon. Spooky riddles. SUMMARY: Witches, skeletons, ghosts, vampires, mummies, and the like are featured in this collection of riddles. 1. Riddles, Juvenile. 2. Supernatural—Anecdotes, facetiae, satire, etc. [1. Riddles. 2. Supernatural—Wit and humor] I. Title. PN6371.5.B76 1983 818'.5402 83-6051 ISBN: 0-394-86093-4 (trade); 0-394-96093-9 (lib. bdg.) Manufactured in the United States of America

27 26 25

W hat does a mother ghost say
to her child when they get
into the car?

Why do skeletons hate winter?

The cold goes right through them.

Why was Dracula put in jail?

He tried to rob a blood bank.

What rides at the amusement park do ghosts like best?

The scary-go-round and
the roller ghoster.

What is the best way
to talk to a ghost?

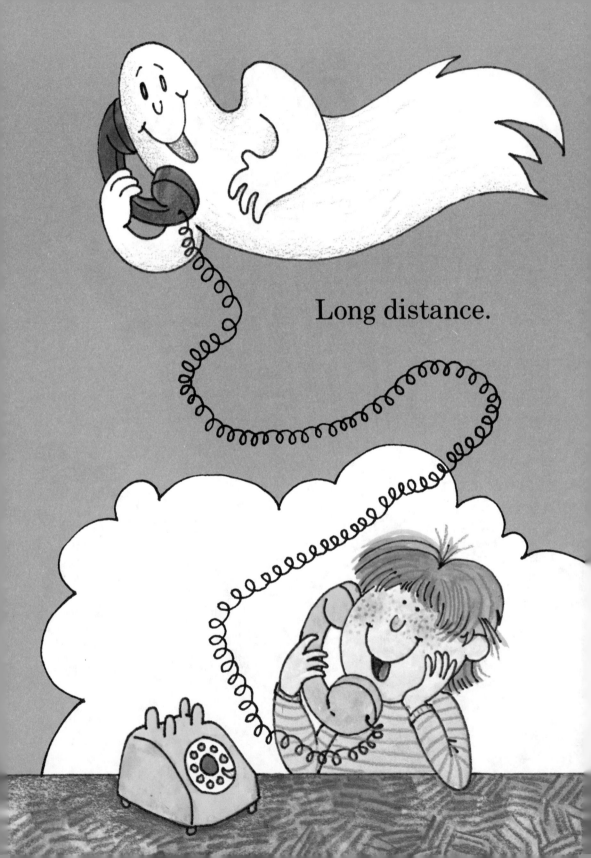

Long distance.

W hat does a witch ask for when she checks into a hotel?

Broom service.

Why do witches fly on brooms?

Vacuum cleaners
are too heavy.

What do bats need after a shower?

A bat mat.

What time is it when a ghost comes to dinner?

Time to go!

What does a little witch hope to get for her birthday?

A haunted dollhouse.

What should you do
when you see a ghost?

Hope the ghost does not see you.

How does a witch tell time?

With a witchwatch.

Why don't skeletons go to scary movies?

They don't have the guts.

Why do vampires drink blood?

What do you call a mummy who eats cookies in bed?

A crummy mummy.

Why do witches
wear pointy hats?

To cover their pointy heads.

What yard will kids never play in?

A graveyard.

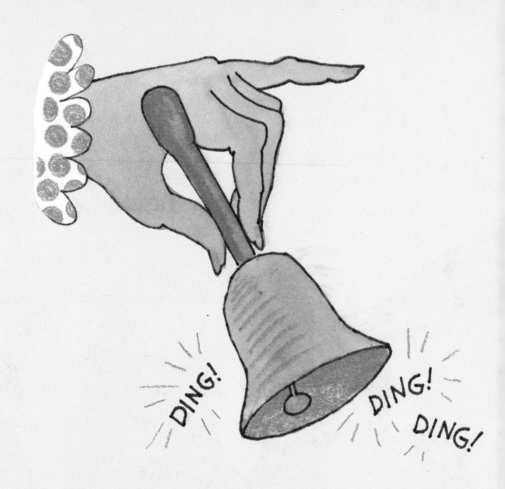

DING! DING! DING!

What do you get when you cross
a bell and a bat?

A dingbat.

What did the detective mummy say when he solved the case of the missing cat?

"That about wraps it up."

Marc Brown grew up in a spooky neighborhood in Mill Creek, Pennsylvania, where there were no streetlights and many of the old houses had secret passageways. Halloween was terribly spooky there, but it is still his favorite holiday. He likes to collect riddles and jokes—spooky and otherwise—as he travels around the country talking to children at schools. He got the idea for a collection of spooky riddles by talking with his son, Tucker.

Marc Brown lives in an eighteenth-century house in Hingham Harbor, Massachusetts, where his two young sons keep him in touch with what children like to read. He is the author of the Bright & Early book *Wings on Things* and many other popular children's books.